UNITED KINGDOM

Sarah Tieck

Big Buddy BOOKS
Explore the Countries

VISIT US AT
www.abdopublishing.com

Published by ABDO Publishing Company, PO Box 398166, Minneapolis, MN 55439.

Printed in the United States of America, North Mankato, Minnesota.
052013
112013

 PRINTED ON RECYCLED PAPER

Coordinating Series Editor: Rochelle Baltzer
Contributing Editors: Megan M. Gunderson, Marcia Zappa
Graphic Design: Adam Craven
Cover Photograph: *Shutterstock*: Patrick Wang.
Interior Photographs/Illustrations: *AP Photo*: Alastair Grant Pool, file (p. 19), Dan Hallman/Invision (p. 33), Lefteris Pitarakis (p. 31), Press Association via AP Images (p. 17), Staff/Worth (p. 15), U.S. Office of War Information (p. 15); *Getty Images*: Daniel Mytens (p. 13), SuperStock (p. 16); *Glow Images*: imagebroker/Josef Beck (p. 29), Gerth Roland (p. 35); *iStockphoto*: ©iStockphoto.com/burcintuncer (p. 11), ©iStockphoto.com/fintastique (p. 29), ©iStockphoto.com/georgeclerk (p. 25), ©iStockphoto.com/imagestock (p. 38), ©iStockphoto.com/majaiva (p. 5), ©iStockphoto.com/northlightimages (p. 25), ©iStockphoto.com/robfordphotography (p. 11), ©iStockphoto.com/stevegeer (p. 23); *Shutterstock*: Aitor Bouzo Ateca (p. 35), Rachelle Burnside (p. 21), Globe Turner (pp. 19, 38), Joe Gough (p. 34), Chris Harvey (p. 9), Stephen Inglis (p. 34), Gail Johnson (p. 35), MagSpace (p. 37), Dmitry Naumov (p. 9), Pixelbliss (p. 27), Mark William Richardon (p. 27), JASON STEEL (p. 23).

Country population and area figures taken from the CIA World Factbook.

Library of Congress Control Number: 2013932177

Cataloging-in-Publication Data

Tieck, Sarah.
  United Kingdom / Sarah Tieck.
    p. cm. -- (Explore the countries)
  ISBN 978-1-61783-819-4 (lib. bdg.)
  1. United Kingdom--Juvenile literature.   I. Title.
  941--dc23
                                                    2013932177

UNITED KINGDOM

Contents

AROUND THE WORLD

Our world has many countries. Each country has beautiful land. It has its own rich history. And, the people have their own languages and ways of life.

The United Kingdom is a country in Europe. What do you know about this country? Let's learn more about this place and its story!

 Did You Know?

English is the official language of the United Kingdom.

Big Ben is a famous clock tower in London. It was completed around 1858.

Passport to the United Kingdom

The United Kingdom is a country in western Europe. It includes England, Scotland, Wales, and Northern Ireland. Some people call it the UK. It is bordered by Ireland, the Atlantic Ocean, and the North Sea.

The UK's total area is 94,058 square miles (243,610 sq km). More than 63 million people live there.

WHERE IN THE WORLD?

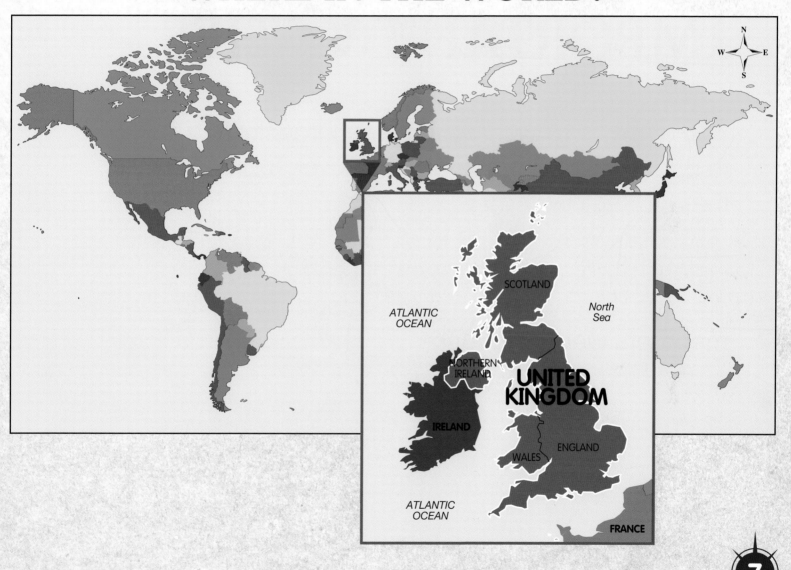

Important Cities

London is the UK's **capital** and largest city. It is home to about 8.2 million people. The River Thames flows through the city.

London was founded in AD 43. The city is filled with historic buildings. The Tower of London was once a prison. Long ago, some of England's royal family members were held there.

SAY IT
Thames
TEHMZ

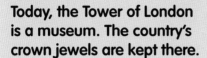

Today, the Tower of London is a museum. The country's crown jewels are kept there.

A glass tower known as "the Gherkin" is easily spotted in London. This modern building looks like a giant gherkin pickle!

Birmingham is the UK's second-largest city. It has about 1.1 million people. This is an important manufacturing area. Car parts, chocolate, jewelry, and other products are made there. The city is also popular with visitors.

Leeds is the UK's third-largest city, with about 750,000 people. Clothing and wool are made there. The city is near important coalfields. And, it is home to the University of Leeds.

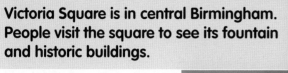

Victoria Square is in central Birmingham. People visit the square to see its fountain and historic buildings.

The River Aire flows through Leeds.

United Kingdom in History

People have lived in what is now the United Kingdom for thousands of years. Different tribes and people settled the land. They brought their own ideas and ways of living. Over time, all of them blended together.

In 1536, England and Wales were **united**. Then in 1707, Scotland joined them. Together, they formed the Kingdom of Great Britain. This meant they shared one government. They worked together and built an **empire**.

King James VI of Scotland became King James I of England in 1603. He helped bring together Scotland and England.

In 1801, Ireland became part of the United Kingdom. By 1900, the UK ruled many parts of the world. But its people struggled during **World War I** and **World War II**.

More and more UK colonies wanted their independence. Australia, Canada, and others had gained independence by 1931. And in 1921, most of Ireland had split from the UK.

By 2000, the UK had lost much of its **empire**. Still, the country was considered important around the world.

During World War II, Germans attacked English cities many times.

Timeline

1746

The Battle of Culloden took place in Scotland's Highlands. It ended an uprising led by Charles Edward Stuart.

About 1000 BC

People began living on Castle Rock in present-day Scotland. Over time, buildings were added to this rock. It became known as Edinburgh Castle.

AD 1558

Elizabeth I became the queen of England. She was one of the country's most famous queens. The time she ruled was known as the Golden Age.

1962

The Beatles recorded their first song. This rock band formed in Liverpool, England. They became world famous.

2012

Queen Elizabeth II celebrated her Diamond Jubilee. This meant she had been queen for 60 years.

1979

Margaret Thatcher became the UK's first female prime minister.

An Important Symbol

The United Kingdom's flag was adopted in 1801. The crosses stand for England, Scotland, and Ireland.

The UK's government is a **constitutional monarchy**. Parliament makes laws. The monarch, or king or queen, is the head of state. The prime minister is the head of government.

The UK's flag is called the Union Jack.

Elizabeth II became the UK's queen in 1952. Her son Prince Charles is next in line to be the king.

ACROSS THE LAND

The United Kingdom's land is on two main islands. It has many upland areas including the Highlands and the Pennines. Scotland is famous for its **moors**. Northern Ireland has low mountains and farmland. Southeast England has hills and flat plains.

The Thames and Severn are the UK's longest rivers. Lough Neagh in Northern Ireland and Loch Lomond in Scotland are large lakes. And, England's Lake District is popular with visitors.

SAY IT

Lough and **Loch**
LAHK

Did You Know?

In January, the average temperature in London is 39°F (4°C). In July, it is 63°F (17°C).

The white cliffs of Dover are along England's southeastern coast.

21

Many types of animals make their homes in the UK. These include rabbits, hares, red deer, pheasants, pigeons, and grouse. Newts, frogs, toads, lizards, and snakes are also common.

The UK's land is home to many different plants. Heather, bluebells, and oak trees are common there.

Did You Know?

Northern Ireland has no wild snakes.

European vipers are poisonous snakes. They are known for the zigzag pattern on their backs and spots on their sides.

Scotland's Highlands are famous for heather. It has many uses. Animals eat it and it has been used to make huts and sheds.

EARNING A LIVING

The United Kingdom makes many products. Its factories produce steel and machines for farming and mining. They also make food products. Some people have jobs in finance, real estate, business, and government. And, many help the country's visitors.

The UK has important natural **resources**. These include oil and natural gas. Farmers produce wheat, barley, sugar beets, apples, cherries, and potatoes. They raise cattle, poultry, and sheep.

Mixed farming is popular in the UK.
Farmers may raise both animals and crops.

The UK is an important European
oil producer. Much of its oil comes
from beneath the North Sea.

Life in the United Kingdom

The UK is known for its beauty and history. It is home to famous artists and writers. Visitors travel from around the world to see its castles, theater plays, and museums.

Traditional foods are often simple. They include fish and chips, mutton, roast beef, and Yorkshire pudding. People drink tea with milk and sugar, as well as beer.

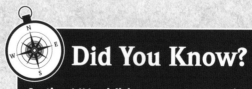

Did You Know?

In the UK, children must attend school from ages 4 or 5 until age 16.

Fish and chips is fried fish and French fries. This may be served with vinegar.

Buckingham Palace is the London home of the UK's royal family.

Soccer, or football, is very popular in the UK. People there also enjoy cricket and rugby. Other favorite activities are hiking, biking, gardening, and hunting. Lawn bowling, or bowls, is also popular.

Religion is important in the UK. Most people belong to either the Church of England or the Church of Scotland. The UK's king or queen is the head of the Church of England.

In 2012, London hosted the Olympic Games. The Olympic rings hung from the Tower Bridge during this event.

Westminster Abbey is a famous church in London. Kings and queens have been crowned there.

Famous Faces

Many talented people are from the UK. William Shakespeare was a famous writer. He was born in 1564 in Stratford-upon-Avon, England.

Many consider Shakespeare the world's greatest playwright, or writer of plays. He wrote *Hamlet*, *Romeo and Juliet*, *Macbeth*, and other famous plays. Shakespeare died in 1616. But, his plays are still popular today.

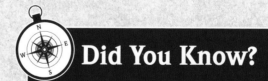

Did You Know?

Many famous sayings are lines from Shakespeare's writing. One of these is "To be, or not to be," from the play *Hamlet*.

Shakespeare wrote more than 150 poems called sonnets.

Joanne Kathleen "J.K." Rowling is one of today's talented writers. She was born on July 31, 1965, in Yate, England. She is famous for writing the popular Harry Potter novels. People around the world love them!

Rowling's Harry Potter books are about a young wizard. She told the story in seven books. The first was printed in 1997. The books were made into eight popular movies.

Tour Book

Have you ever been to the United Kingdom? If you visit the country, here are some places to go and things to do!

 ## See

Visit Stonehenge in southern England. No one knows why this ancient stone circle was built. Some people believe it was a place of worship.

 ## Explore

Visit Giant's Causeway on the northern coast of Northern Ireland. The unusual rock shapes formed from lava flows.

 # Climb

Hike in Snowdonia National Park in Wales. At 3,560 feet (1,085 m), Snowdon is the highest mountain in England and Wales.

 # Swim

Check out the Fairy Pools on the Isle of Skye in Scotland. They are known for their clear water and beauty. Even though they are cold, many people swim in them!

 # Watch

Spend time near Loch Ness in the Scottish Highlands. This deep lake is said to be home to the Loch Ness Monster.

A Great Country

The story of the United Kingdom is important to our world. The people and places that make up this country offer something special. They help make the world a more beautiful, interesting place.

Scotland's Highlands are famous for their history, beauty, and castles.

United Kingdom Up Close

Official Name: United Kingdom of Great Britain and Northern Ireland

Flag:

Population (rank): 63,047,162
(July 2012 est.)
(22nd most-populated country)

Total Area (rank): 94,058 square miles
(80th largest country)

Capital: London

Official Language: English

Currency: British pound

Form of Government: Constitutional monarchy

National Anthem: "God Save the Queen" (or "God Save the King")

Important Words

capital a city where government leaders meet.

constitutional monarchy a form of government in which a king or queen has only those powers given by a country's laws and constitution.

empire a large group of states or countries under one ruler called an emperor or empress.

moor open land with poor farming soil.

resource a supply of something useful or valued.

unite to come together for purpose or action.

World War I a war fought in Europe from 1914 to 1918.

World War II a war fought in Europe, Asia, and Africa from 1939 to 1945.

Web Sites

To learn more about the United Kingdom, visit ABDO Publishing Company online. Web sites about the United Kingdom are featured on our Book Links page. These links are routinely monitored and updated to provide the most current information available.

www.abdopublishing.com

Index